Living To Satisfaction As If Each Of Our Days Are Numbered And Coping With Trying Times

Raekwon Williams

Living To Satisfaction As If Each Of Our Days Are Numbered And Coping With Trying Times

Copyright © 2022 by Raekwon M. Williams

The following is a work of fiction. Names, characters, places, and incidents are a representation of the author's imagination. Any resemblance to actual people, living or dead, or to businesses, companies, events, and institutions is completely coincidental.

Paperback ISBN- 978-0-578-28366-1

Hardcover ISBN- 978-0-578-29044-7

Ebook ISBN- 9798201487928

All rights reserved. No Part of this publication may be reproduced, scanned, or transmitted in any form, digital or printed, without the written consent of the author.

Contents

Introduction..5.

The Gift Of A Wrestler.. 6.

Stick Tight To Your Family And Friends……………………………………………. 9.

Always Be Prepared……………………………………………………….. 12.

When Will It End…………………………………………………… 16.

Peforming With No Crowd……………………………………………. 19 .

The Evil Storm…………………………………………………………….. 23.

Living With No Fear…………………………………………………. 27.

Why Blame The Year………………………………………………. 30.

Never Take Anything For Granted With Anyone…………………………………. 34.

Making It To 21……………………………………………………………….. 38.

Unitied We Stay……………………………………………………………… 41.

Until We Meet Again………………………………………………………… 45.

Closing Remarks…………………………………………………………….. 47.

Introduction

It's not easy having to live in this current world because it's filled with hardships. The darkness that surrounds us often obscures the light, but there is light at the end of the tunnel. It's a matter of looking at everything as it is. When it comes to things that we cannot control, like a pandemic or natural disaster, or when our lives take a surprising turn, sometimes we have no choice but to face the music. It's not easy to shake off the effects of such things, but what can be done is look back on our past experiences to determine how we've been living. Have we spent too much time away from our families and friends?

Have we taken proper precautions before important tasks needed to be accomplished? Have we ever stopped to think of the possibility of not being able to travel to some of the places we love for a while? As a matter of fact, no such questions should be asked in our mines after a storm hits such as a pandemic or when our lives hit rock bottom. Instead, we tend to overlook the things we have by taking them for granted. We can live to satisfaction by never taking anything for granted and being thankful for the people that we have left.

Living gracefully means not focusing on what we lost or what we ought to have done, but rather clinging to the people we've left and never taking anything for granted. We can live graciously when we cling to those we love. We must stay united, not be driven by fear, and hold on to our loved ones closer now than ever before. When we live this way, we can cope with these tough times more easily since we can focus on the positives instead of the negatives. We must remember that nobody is guaranteed life. We should therefore value ourselves, value our relationships, stop blaming the year, and value what we have.

The Gift Of A Wrestler

Some days I feel like riding on a bicycle at full speed without anybody telling me to break free.

Some days I feel like riding on a horse with so much force it's as if I'm sprinting beyond a course.

Some days I feel like riding in my car taking a nice road trip without a muscle from my body ripping me apart.

Some days I feel like going to an island sitting there peacefully without anyone breaking my silence.

Some days I feel like going on a cruise with no fear of getting seasick because it won't lay a feather on my groove.

Some days I feel like flying to Hawaii with no need to feel the breeze because the wind would be blowing all over me.

Some days I feel like going ice skating with no fear of falling because it's only my first date.

Some days I feel like surfing without any thoughts of the waves taking me to the deep end.

Some days I feel like going to the beach with the heat and the sand being no match for me.

I got the gift of a wrestler; I'm never going to stop.

I got the gift of a wrestler; nothing can take me apart.

I got the gift of a wrestler; I'm going to keep reaching to the top.

I got the gift of a wrestler; I never stop fighting.

I got the gift of a wrestler; I fight until the end.

I got the gift of a wrestler; I body slam the evil voices from within

I got the gift of a wrestler; I take more risk.

I got the gift of a wrestler; I take more chances.

I got the gift of a wrestler; I take every day of my life as if It's the last one that I got left.

I got the gift of a wrestler, I put negativity into a submission hold.

I got the gift of a wrestler; I don't wait for storylines to unfold.

I got the gift of a wrestler; I'm filled with positive vibes and when that bell rings, I'm ready to knock down anything that comes between my vibes.

Stick Tight To Your Family And Friends

Why should you smile if one of your parents enters your room?

Why should you dance when your friends call your phone?

Why should you sing when your parents call your name?

Why should you feel warm when your mom wants a long hug?

Why should you feel hot when your dad wants to go to the basketball court?

Why should you feel energetic when your friends want to hang in the middle of the night?

Why should you run into your mother's arms when she wants a big kiss?

Why should you jump on your grandma's back when she feeds you loads of food?

Why should you tell your mama that you love her even after she's told you 5 million times?

Stick tight to your family and friends because their time will end.

Stick tight to your family and friends because tomorrow is never promised.

Stick tight to your family and friends just as the rain sticks with wind.

Stick tight to your family and friends, hold onto to them like a feather on a pen.

Stick tight to your family and friends, enjoy your time with them as if the world's going to end.

Stick tight to your family and friends, time is precious and can never be brought back.

Stick tight to your family and friends, laugh with them as much as you can or forever hold your peace.

Stick tight to your family and friends, give them more love than you ever have before.

Stick tight to your family and friends because on any given day their time can end.

Always Be Prepared

Why do we buy groceries once we are running low?

Why do we only get gas when our car is nearly on E?

Why do we exercise when our health is low?

Why do we still buy winter clothes in the spring?

Why do we buy bug spray for our house when bugs have already come in?

Why do we pay our bills on the day of the deadline?

Why do we only come together as a family when someone has died?

Why do we only call our loved ones when one of them are sick?

Why do we embrace at the worst times rather than the better?

Why do we sleep when we should be awake?

Why are we awake when we should be sleep?

Why do we turn off our lights when a storm is coming?

Why do we study the night before a test?

Why do we save money when we have very little left?

Why do we only clean when germs are spreading the surfaces?

We should always be prepared for anything.

Always be prepared to buy groceries even before your completely out.

Always be prepared to get gas even before your car goes on E.

Always be prepared to exercise even when you're in good health.

Always be prepared to switch clothes before spring in your house.

Always be prepared to buy bug spray even before bugs arrive.

Always be prepared to pay bills days before the deadline.

Always be prepared to come together with family.

Always be prepared to call your loved ones thru thick and then.

Always be prepared to always embrace.

Always be prepared to stay awake.

Always be prepared to sleep when necessary.

Always be prepared to save electricity even before a storm.

Always be prepared to study days before a test.

Always be prepared to save money even when you've a lot more.

Always be prepared to be clean even when it's not that dirty.

Always be prepared for anything that comes your way.

Always be prepared because life can strike you on any given day.

When Will It End?

When will we leave the house of boredom?

When will we feel the breeze of air?

When will we open the door of wind?

When will we go to family gatherings?

When will we go to stores without mask?

When will we see our friends again?

When will we be able to scream at concerts?

When will we watch our sports in peace?

When will we go to work again?

When will we swim in the water like fish?

When will we go back to amusement parks?

When will we travel again?

When will schools reopen?

When will trains cross the tracks?

When will we meet face to face again?

When will we stop working virtually?

When will we stop doing school virtually?

When will the virtual world come to an end?

When will we eat inside restaurants?

When will we order food inside fast-food places?

When will we eat out again?

One day this will end.

One day our life's will be reborn.

One day we will hold hands as a family again.

That day will come, but it is unknown.

That day we will walk on earth like we never had before.

That day we will sing as if it's a sunny day.

When will it end? We don't know.

One day it will end, but that day has yet to come.

Until that day comes, we must have faith within our hearts that this will all fade away.

Performing With No Crowd

Imagine if one day all your fans were gone.

All the seats were empty without a sound of the thunderous noise that you are used to hearing.

There's not a single voice or echo vibrating thru the arena.

It is so empty that not even the sound of cracks could be heard.

There's no screaming insight.

There are no fans cheering your glorious name.

Is this a dream? Is it a dream that everything is empty?

Is it your conscious mind that is fooling you from the reality?

Are your fans really gone or is it just all in your head?

Are you really stepping on stage with no crowd, or do you believe that the crowd is always there?

Are you really singing, dancing, or acting on stage in peer silence or do the noise vibrate into your own mind?

Are you really performing alone on stage, or can you picture others performing with you?

The reality is this is not a fantasy, you are performing with no crowd.

How should you feel or how should you think?

Should you feel like the grass when there's no rain?

Should you feel frighten that you can only hear your own voice?

Should you feel happy that millions of your fans aren't cheering your glorious name?

However, you may feel the reality is in your face because there is no crowd.

You are not dreaming, and you are not fantasizing

What should you do?

You should perform like you are your own crowd.

You should utilize this opportunity because your days are limited, and it won't come back.

You should perform at your best because your screaming fans are there.

Your fans are not there physically, but they are there in your heart.

Performing with no crowd is like performing with one.

You control the pace, the tempo, and the speed of your agility.

No one can dictate how fast you should go because your all alone.

You should perform with no crowd as if your lives depend on it.

Soon the loud thunderous noise of the crowd will come back, and you'll have more energy to perform like you never had before.

The Evil Storm

When we wake up, the storm is there.

When we close our eyes, the storm is there.

When we sleepwalk in the middle of the night, the storm is there.

When we go to the store, the storm is there.

When we try to travel, the storm is there.

When we step outside, the storm is there.

When we want to hug our friends, the storm is there.

When we want to hug family, the storm is there.

When we want to see our family, the storm is there.

When we want to go to the beach, the storm is there.

When we want to get a tan, the storm is there.

When we want to wave hello, the storm is there.

When we go to our essential jobs, the storm is there.

When we want to get a car wash, the storm is there.

When we come home from work, the storm is there.

There's not a day on the news where the evil storm isn't mentioned.

This evil storm forces us to wear mask wherever we go.

This evil storm forces us to breathe less because it's airborne.

This evil storm is stronger than the actual weather.

This evil storm can cause more deaths than a hurricane.

This evil storm is bigger than a tornado but weakens in the heat.

This evil storm can strike us faster than lightning.

This evil storm is like a lion chasing us at full speed.

This evil storm is more powerful than anything we've seen before.

This evil storm may have caused us to stay distance.

This evil storm may have taken away some of our loved ones.

This evils storm may have forced us to not go certain places.

But this evil storm won't take away our pride.

This evil storm won't take away our spirit.

If we stay positive, we can make it through the evil storm.

There have been many evil storms before, and this is just another phrase.

We must not let this storm get to us and be thankful that we are still here.

We must stay strong, and we must stay positive because with our strength, the evil storm will eventually go away.

Living With No Fear

Why should we fear being stuck at home?

Why should we fear being paid less than before?

Why should we fear travel restriction from our loved ones far gone?

Why should we fear giving air hugs to one another?

Why should we fear giving fist bumps?

Why should we fear washing our hands more times than before?

Why should we fear standing 6ft apart?

Why should we fear being cleaner?

Why should we fear being clean at all?

Why should we fear going to the drive thru?

Why should we fear wearing mask?

Why should we fear anything that protects us from the evil storm?

Why should we fear watching movies from home?

Why should we fear watching plays from home?

Why should we fear hanging with less people when more will rock your head like a stone?

We shouldn't fear these things, we should be fearless.

We should live with no fear and live our lives to the bone.

We should live our lives to the fullest like we never had before.

Why should we fear something, we can't control?

The evil storm will keep riding by, but fear will only allow it to hurt us more.

Being afraid will drive us apart but having no fear will drive us closer together

We should cling our family and friends just as the eclipse of the moon and the sun.

We should cling them while we have them whether we see them or not.

We should call them more than the grass calls for rain.

We should be living with no fear because the evil storm will end and being fearless will conquer the evil voices that we have within

Why Blame The Year

When someone dies from a stroke, we blame the year.

When someone dies from a heart attack, we blame the year.

When someone dies from cancer, we blame the year.

When someone dies from a car accident, we blame the year.

When someone dies from a plane crash, we blame the year.

When someone dies from drowning, we blame the year.

When someone dies from being shot, we blame the year.

When someone dies from being stab, we blame the year.

When someone dies from natural causes, we blame the year.

When lockdown started, we blamed the year.

When mask was required, we blamed the year.

When large gatherings were cut down to 20, we blamed the year.

When we lost our jobs, we blamed the year.

When we had to file for unemployment, we blamed the year.

When we started working virtually, we blamed the year.

When were stuck with little to go, we blame the year?

When we can't see all our loved ones, we blame the year.

When people die from this evil storm, we blame the year.

Why do we blame the year for these deaths?

Why do we blame the year for these misfortunes?

Why do we blame the year for any of this at all?

No year is ever great, every year there's more at stake.

A year doesn't control the world, but human activity does.

There was never a perfect year from the beginning of mankind.

People die every day, the year itself has no say.

We must cling our family and friends until there time is no more.

The year didn't bring the storm, we awaken it, now this storm may stay past this year and beyond.

Why blame the year when the year can't walk.

Why blame the year when the year can't talk.

Why blame the year when it's just a cycle of life.

We can't blame the year for the existence of the storm.

We can't blame the year for the hard times that we face.

We can't blame the year for the mental breakdowns that we may have beating within our bones.

The year is just an extension of time. But the storm has no time, so when the storm finally ends, it will feel like an angel coming from the sky.

Never Take Anything For Granted With Anyone

Every moment, every hour we lose someone we love.

Every moment, every hour we should not blame the year.

Every moment, every hour we should be more prepared.

Every moment, every hour we debate over wearing mask.

Every moment, every hour the mask becomes a blast.

Every moment, every hour social distancing is beyond our past.

Every moment, every hour we complain about our little siblings.

Every moment, every hour our little siblings want us nearby.

Every moment, every hour we should hold our little siblings like a bear.

Every moment, every hour the leaves fall from the trees.

Every moment, every hour we become sicklier.

Every moment, every hour we should hang with family and friends while were free.

Every moment, every hour our friends may call our names.

Every moment, every hour we should not try to escape.

Every moment, every hour our friends become beautiful horses that we should never stop riding.

Every moment, every hour our romantic partner becomes a pain.

Every moment, every hour without the pain were not the same.

Every moment, every hour we should love the pain they bring.

Every moment, every hour we want to be alone.

Every moment, every hour our loneliness feels like a stone.

Every moment, every hour we should pick up the phone.

Every moment, every hour the evil storm keeps going.

Every moment, every hour we should live with no fear.

Every moment, every hour no fear grows like a spear.

Never take any moment for granted with anyone because it only comes once.

Never take any moment for granted with anyone because if they leave, you'll be in a slump.

Never take any moment for granted with anyone because your loneliness may put you in a dump.

Never take any moment for granted with anyone because if they leave there is no turning back.

Never take any moment for granted with anyone because you don't want nightmares full of attacks.

Never take any moment for granted with anyone because the risk is full of setbacks.

Never take any moment for granted with anyone because the hours don't want big mistakes.

Never take any moment for granted with anyone because if they leave of if they die your life maybe at stake.

Never take any moment for granted with anyone because you want to keep sailing forward in life and not sailing back deep into the waters.

Making It To 21

Sometimes we take our age for granted.

Sometimes we overlook our age as just a number.

Sometimes we don't appreciate living up to a certain age.

Sometimes we think living up to age 13 is normal.

Sometimes we think living up to age 16 is normal.

Sometimes we think living up to age 18 is normal.

Did the poor infants think it was normal to die before they were even one?

Did the poor children that battled with cancer think it was normal to die before they were even five?

Did the babies and children think it was normal to lose their lives before it really begun?

What about the youths that were murdered before they were thirteen?

What about the youths that passed away from a car crash before they were sixteen?

What about the youths that died from something as deadly as the evil storm before they were eighteen?

Many of these youths couldn't experience what it's like to be a child.

Many of these youths couldn't experience what it's like to be a teenager.

None of these youths were able to experience what it's like to be an adult.

Making it to 21 is never a guarantee.

Making it to 21 is an age that we are fortunate to be.

Making it to 21 is more of a blessing than it seems.

If we make it to be 21, we've finally approached our adult life.

If we make it to be 21, you can cut the tension within a knife.

If we make it to be 21, there's so much to see in sight.

If we make it to be 21, it should feel as sweet as a candy apple.

If we make it to be 21, it should feel like we hit the jackpot.

If we make it to be 21, it should feel like a phrase of our lives has been complete.

If we make it to be 21, we should be thankful and grateful

If we make it to be 21, we shouldn't look at it as a sin.

If we make it to be 21, we shouldn't underestimate how far we've come and how much further we plan on going.

United We Stay

There's no need to hold a grudge over something small that happened years ago.

Often, some of us find ourselves distancing from our family members giving them the silent treatment.

Yet the same group of us who stopped speaking to them find ourselves saddened when they die or are on their death bed.

Why didn't we feel that way when we had years to make up?

Should the death of that person be a wakeup call?

Should it be a wake-up call to let go of a small argument or disagreement?

It should never be that way, but some of us find ourselves in that trap.

Is there a way to avoid that trap? Of course, it is and that is to resolve such minor issues.

Perhaps this worldwide evil storm is a perfect example of how quickly we can lose a family member within just one day.

So, if the issue is small, we must resolve the matter among each other because family is all you got.

Surely, we have close friends who we may have small conflicts with, but just like family, we must cling to them.

If we cling to our family and friends then we won't feel guilt when they are gone, so united we stay.

United we stay when small conflicts occur between us and our loved ones because we may not see them again.

United we stay when we face the daily challenge everyday of leaving our homes to go to work or run errands with the possibility of never coming back.

United we stay when whether we have the shot or not, the evil storm is still as strong as it was when it first begun. Social distancing is still important.

We must stay united and not remain bitter against our loved ones over a small cup of tea.

There's a difference between forgiving and holding a grudge, but some of us find ourselves remaining in the trap of a grudge.

We can forgive someone family or not without associating with them if what they have done was severe and if they ignore us no matter what we do.

Most of the time the issues aren't to that level, so we must stay united and not hold onto the past.

United we stay with all our loved ones because you reap what you sow and if we don't stay united the guilt will harm you for years to come.

Until We Meet Again (In dedication to a friend of mines who passed away)

I can hear your voice; I can hear your voice whispering in my ear.

I can hear the way your voice sounded every time you used to sing.

I can still remember the times that we danced, sang, and laughed together just as friends should.

You were the closest wrestling teammate that I ever had, and with you now being gone from my presence it hurts me in ways that I can't explain.

I have faith that one day you and I will see each other again. Maybe not in this current system of things, but in the new world that will follow, we will soon meet again.

No longer would I have to shed a tear thinking about your existence.

No longer would I have to picture an image of times we wrestled each other doing practices.

No longer would I have to picture the times we danced together no matter where we went or sang together like there was no tomorrow.

When that time comes, I won't have to glance at your glorious memories.

When that time comes, we'll just have fun together just as we did before.

This time it'll be stronger than it was before and until we meet again all these things will be beyond my imagination.

One day we'll meet again, and until we meet again your memories will stay in me forever.

Closing remarks- The last peace in this book is dedicated to a friend of mine who passed away too soon. His memories will forever remain in my heart forever and I will never forget him. In the same way that he will forever be glued into my heart, let us all continue to create memories with our loved ones still standing.

www.ingramcontent.com/pod-product-compliance
Lightning Source LLC
Chambersburg PA
CBHW070519090426
42735CB00012B/2845